a @lavenderandsilkpublishing

E LavenderandSilk

◉ @lavenderandsilkpublishing

All rights reserved. No part of this book may be reproduced in any form. This includes information storage and commercial distribution without the permission of @lavenderandsilkpublishing

Disclaimer!

Words of affirmation is my dominant love language by an embarrassing mile. So, I wanted to create a book full of reminders that helped me during my weepy and tender moments. My hope is that, by sharing them, they might offer you some solace too.

I am not a scholar of Islamic sciences, hadith, or fiqh, nor have I devoted years to academic study. This is simply a compilation of Islamic reflections that have dropped into my heart at some point or another.

I have done my best to credit and reference every reminder, with full Harvard citations included at the back of the book. If you notice any errors please reach out, and I will correct them immediately.

Thank you for your patience and understanding.

@lavenderandsilkpublishing

Chapter One:
Direct from the Golden Source.

Chapter Two:
Allah (swt) Mercy.

Chapter Three:
Emotional Intelligence.

Chapter Four:
Staying Hopeful.

Chapter One

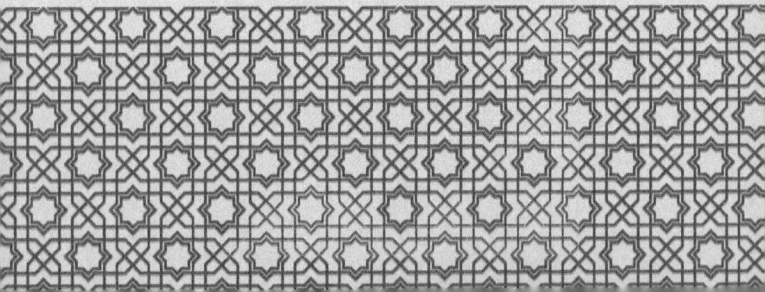

Direct from the
Golden Source

God does not wish to place any burden on you: He only wishes to cleanse you and perfect His blessing on you, so that you may be thankful.

SURAH MA'IDAH
5:6

... If Allah finds any goodness in your hearts He will give you that which is better than what has been taken away from you, and He will forgive you. Allah is Ever-Forgiving, Most Merciful.

SURAH AL-ANFAL
8:70

And by the Mercy of God, you dealt with them gently. Had you been severe and harsh-hearted, they would have broken away from about you; so pass over (their faults), and ask (Allah's) Forgiveness for them...

SURAH ALI-IMRAN
3:159

You are not (able) to frustrate (Allah) neither in the earth nor in the sky. And, apart from Allah, you have neither a protector nor a helper.

SURAH AL'ANKABUT
29:22

Call upon Me and I will respond to You.

SURAH GHAFIR
40:60

It is He who sent down tranquility into the hearts of the believers that they would increase in faith ...

SURAH AL-FATH
48:4

And We already created man and know what his soul whispers to him, and We are closer to him than (his) jugular vein.

SURAH QAF
50:16

... Surely, your Rubb is liberal in forgiving. He knows you well. He created you from dust and when you were foetus in the wombs of your mothers. Therefore, do not justify your purity. He knows well who are the pious.

SURAH AN-NAJM
53:32

He created the heavens and the earth with truth, and He shaped you. Then perfected your forms in beauty. To Him is the ultimate return.

SURAH AT-TAGHABUN
64:3

Do not let their words sadden you ...

SURAH YUNUS
10:65

What is with you shall perish and what is with Allah shall last. And certainly, We shall bless those who observed patience, with their reward for the best of what they used to do.

SURAH AN-NAHAL
16:96

The servants of the Rahman (the All Merciful, Allah) are those who walk on the earth humbly and when the ignorant people speak to them, they reply peacefully.

SURAH AL-FURQAN
25:63

So, be patient. Surely Allah's promise is true, and let not the disbelievers shake your firmness.

SURAH AR-RUM
30:60

... and be patient over what befalls upon you. Surely, these are affairs which require courage and determination.

SURAH LUQMAN
31:17

... but pursue for peace for you will have the upper hand as Allah is with you ...

SURAH MUHAMMAD
47:35

If you lend Allah a good loan He will multiply it for you and forgive you. For Allah is the Most Appreciative, Most Forbearing.

SURAH AT-TAGHABUN
64:17

And bear patiently all that they say and go apart from them gracefully.

SURAH AL-MUZZAMMIL
73:10

By the morning brightness, And (by) the night when it covers with darkness, Your Rubb has not left you, nor He is displeased with you, And the Hour which follows is better for you than the previous moments.

SURAH AD-DUHAA
93:1-4

Verily, in the remembrance of Allah
do hearts find rest.

SURAH AR-RAD
13:28

If you are grateful I will surely give you more.

SURAH IBRAHIM
14:7

And He gave you everything
you asked for. And if you
count the favours of Allah, you
cannot count them ...

SURAH IBRAHIM
14:34

Never stretch your eyes towards what We have given to groups of them to enjoy, and do not grieve for them, and be kind to believers in humbleness.

SURAH AL-HIJR
15:88

And Allah has created you from
the womb of your mothers
while you knew nothing. And
gave you ears and eyes and
hearts so that you may be
thankful.

SURAH AN-NAHL
16:78

... Do good to others as God
has done good to you ...

SURAH AL-QASAS
28:77

...Anyone who is grateful
does so to the profit of his
own soul...

SURAH LUQMAN
31:12

And in their wealth there was a right of the needy and the deprived.

SURAH ADH-DHARIYAT
51:19

Limitless is your Lord in His Mercy.

SURAH AL-AN'AM
6:147

Show forgiveness, speak for justice
and avoid the ignorant.

SURAH AL-ARAF
7:199

And If they incline towards
peace, then you also incline to it
and put trust in Allah. Surely,
He is the Hearing, Knowing.

SURAH AL-ANFAL
8:61

And seek forgiveness from your Lord; then turn to Him wholeheartedly. Verily, my Lord is Merciful, Most Loving.

SURAH HUD
11:90

And it is out of His mercy that He has made day and night for you, so that you may have rest in it, and so that you may search for His grace and so that you may be grateful.

SURAH AL-QASAS
28:73

.... do not despair of Allah's mercy. Surely, Allah will forgive all sins. Surely, He is the One who is the Most- Forgiving, the Very Merciful.

SURAH AZ-ZUMAR
39:53

It may be that you hate
something and it is good
for you and it may be that
you love something and it
is bad for you.

SURAH BAQARAH
2:216

and (for those who) when they
get angry, they forgive.

SURAH ASH-SHURAA
42:37

God will find a way out for those who are mindful of Him, And He will provide him from (sources) he never could imagine. And whosoever puts his trust in Allah, then He will suffice him. God will accomplish His purpose. God has appointed a measure of time for everything.

SURAH AT-TALAQ
65:2-3

... Tell me, if Allah takes away your hearing and your sights and sets a seal on your heart, which God other than Allah can bring these back to you?

SURAH AL-AN'AM
6:46

If they intend to deceive you,
then Allah is sufficient for you.
It is He who gave you strength ...

SURAH AL-ANFAL
8:62

Do you not see how Allah compares a good word to a good tree? It's root is firm and it's branches reach the sky?

SURAH IBRAHIM
14:24

If all the trees on earth
become pens, and the sea
replenished by seven more
seas were to supply them with
ink, the Words of Allah
would not be exhausted ...

SURAH LUQMAN
31:27

My Lord, put my heart at peace for me.

SURAH TAHA
20:25

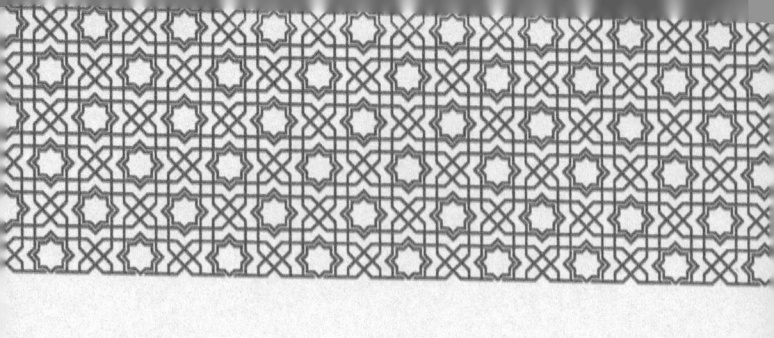

Chapter Two

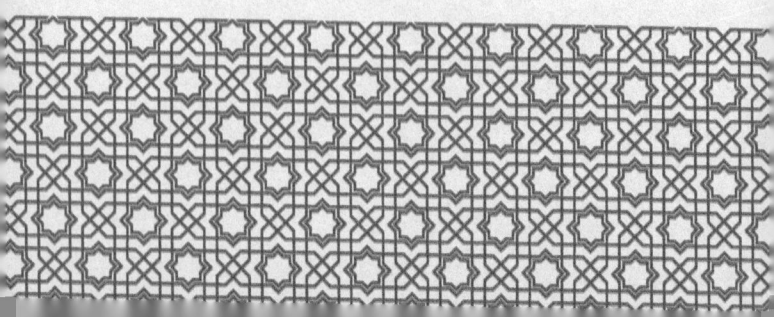

Allah's (swt) Mercy

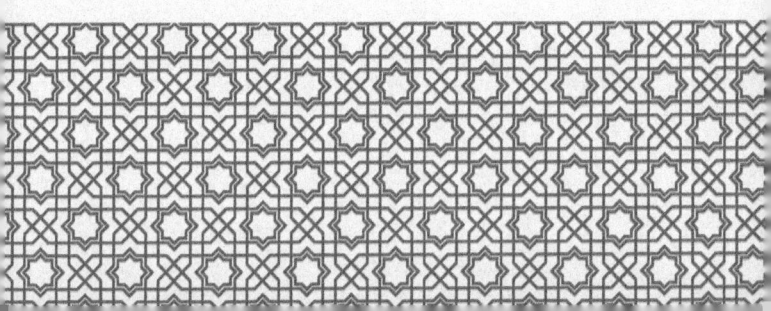

Rahman and Rahim both come from the same Arabic root, ra-ha-min, which means a combination of tenderness, affection, sympathy and compassion. In showing us what this looks like in action, the Prophet (pbuh) pointed to a scene that was occurring right before the Companions eyes:

A women was frantically looking for her child in the aftermath of a battle. Imagine the feeling of a mother who, for one moment, thinks she had lost her child, and in the battlefield. Imagine her feeling when she finally found him, scooped him up and wept, and then nursed him. After witnessing this scene, the Prophet (pbuh) asked his Companions. 'Do you think that this woman would throw her child in the fire?' And they said' No, by God she would not, If she is able not to.' He then said. 'Allah the Exalted is more merciful with His slave then this woman with her child.'

Jinan Yousef (2023) p.24-25

It is not allowed for anyone to loose hope in Allah's Mercy, even if his sins are very great.

Ibn Taymiyyah.

Abu Huraira reported: I heard Allah's Messenger (may peace be upon him) as saying:

Allah created mercy in one hundred parts and He retained with Him ninety-nine parts, and He has sent down upon the earth one part, and it is because of this one part that there is mutual love among the creation so much so that the animal lifts up its hoof from its young one, fearing that it might harm it.

Sahih Muslim (6629)

When one of you loves his brother, let him know.

Sunan Abī Dāwūd (5124)

The Prophet (pbuh) said.

Allah Almighty said:
O son of Adam, if you call upon Me and place your hope in Me; I will forgive you without hesitation.

O son of Adam, if you have sins pilling up to the clouds and then ask for My forgiveness, I will forgive you without hesitation.

O son of Adam, if you come to Me with enough sins to fill the earth and then you meet Me without associating anything with Me, I will come to you with enough forgiveness to fill the earth.

Jami' at-Tirmidhi 3540)

Ibn Abbas narrated: Once I was in a state of itikaaf in the Prophet's Mosque (Medina). A certain person came to me and sat down. I said to him 'O so and so, you look sad'. He said, 'Yes of course'

So-and-so has his due on me, and by the one who lies in eternal peace in the grave (i.e. Prophet Muhammad), I am not able to pay the debt' I said, 'Should I not talk to him about your debt?' He said, 'You can do so if you like'

There upon I put my shoes on and went out of the mosque. The person asked him, 'Have you forgotten the state you were in (i.e. itikaaf)?' I replied, 'Not at all, but I have heard from the one who lies in eternal peace in the grave [saying this his eyes became filled with tears], said:

"One who moves to fulfill any need of his brother, and makes effort for it, will find it better than itikaaf of ten years; and one who performs itikaaf for one day for the pleasure of Allah, he will create a distance of three ditches between him and the hell - and each ditch has a width which lies between East and West, or between the heaven and earth."

- 1 ditch = space between the heaven and the earth
- 1 itikaaf = 3 ditches
- one deed of helping someone = 10 years of itikaaf

Al Targhib v.2, p.227

Some people walk on this earth, around you, near you, speaking with you - but they've already been written as a person of Paradise.

Maybe for giving a thirsty dog some water. Maybe for helping a child who was crying. Maybe for tending to a sick person.

And they have their own fears and tears and anxiety and guilt and don't know where they stand.

But they're roaming this earth, on it but not of it. Tending a garden but destined for The Garden. And only God knows who they are.

Maryam Amir.

A mother visited Aisha, may Allah be pleased with her, and was given three dates by Aisha. She gave one date to each of her two children, who then looked at her for the last date. The mother then split the last date in half and gave it to her children. Aisha related this incident to the Prophet (pbuh) who praised the women and said she has entered Paradise because of her just and merciful actions.

Omar Sulieman, 2020, p.25.

One of the Companions, who led the others in prayer during travels, always recited Surat al-Ikhlas. He was asked why he would recite this chapter so frequently. He replied, 'It is because this chapter describes the Most Merciful, and therefore I love to recite it.' When he heard the man's reply, the Prophet (pbuh) said: 'Tell that man that God loves him.' [Bukhari and Muslim}

In another narration, a man said, 'O Messenger of Allah, I love this chapter, 'Say: "He is Allah, the One"'' [112:1] The Messenger of Allah (pbuh) said, 'Your love for it will admit you into Paradise.'

Jinan Yousef (2023) p.149

Sometimes I think of all the invisible people living their untold stories, their untold compromises, and their untold hardships that they are too afraid or ashamed to share with anyone.

Things that are heavy on the heart but frustratingly enough, come out petty and meaningless when spoken out loud. The unshareable.

Things that can only be bled out in poetry, or wept out in prayer. The world is so full of noise. But if you can hear and sense the unshareable in someone, can you also think of a way to comfort them?

Perhaps that's possible. And perhaps someone will comfort you as well. There's a way to feel your way around the invisible, the untold. To hold its heart to your heart.

themusingmulsim.

Your Lord Allah is the Possessor of Modesty and He is Generous. When His servant reaches out to Him with outstretched hands, He feels ashamed to leave that servant with nothing.

Sunan al-Tirmidhi (3556)

The Prophet (pbuh) said.

Allah says, 'If My slave intends to do a bad deed then (O Angels) do not write it until he does it; if he does it, then write it as it is, but if he refrains from doing it for My Sake, then write it as a good deed.

If he intends to do a good deed, but does not do it, then write a good deed, and if he does it, then write it for him as ten good deeds up to seven hundred times.

Sahih al-Bukhari (7501)

Therefore if the pains of this
world tire you, do not grieve.

For it may be that Allah wishes
to hear your voice by of du'a.

blessedexpressions.

Allah (swt) never takes anything away, expect that He replaces it with something better. Reflect on the foetus in the womb, it's nourishment comes from the umbilical cord as a single pathway.

And then once the child is born, he is cut off from that pathway and then the two pathways of milk are open. Once the child is weaned and the two pathways of milk are cut off, four paths are open that are even better for him.

The meat of animals, crops, fresh water and pure milk and diary. And once that person dies those four paths are closed off and Allah (swt) opens the 8 gates of Jannah instead.

Omar Suliman, ep.3 Ramadan 2024 series.

The Prophet (pbuh) said:

Allah does not give someone five things until He has prepared another five things for him.

He does not give him gratitude except that He has prepared for him an increase [in provision and sustenance]

He does not give him supplication (du a') except that He has prepared its award.

He does not give him the asking for forgiveness (istighfar) except that He has prepared for him forgiveness.

He does not give him the asking for repentance except that He has prepared for him acceptance.

And He does not give him charity except that He has prepared for him its reward.

Ibn Hajar Al Asqalani.

I live in the thought of My servant and I am with him as he remembers Me. (The Holy Prophet) further said: By Allah, Allah is more pleased with the repentance of His servant than what one of you would do on finding the lost camel in the waterless desert. When he draws near Me by the span of his hand. I draw near him by the length of a cubit and when he draws near Me by the length of a cubit. I draw near him by the length of a fathom and when he draws near Me walking I draw close to him hurriedly.

Sahih Muslim (2675)

For whomever the door of du'a opened,
for him the doors of mercy are opened.

Tirmidhi (3548)

There are two main things you have to do. The first is to move your heart from dwelling on the things of this world and move it to dwell on the Hereafter, then focus all your heart on the Qur'an and ponder its meanings and why it was revealed.

Try to understand something from every ayah and apply it to the disease of your heart. These ayat were revealed (to treat) the disease of the heart, so you will be healed, by the permission of Allah.

Ibn al-Qayyim on curing one's heart.

Please Allah, protect, help and guide every person that has crossed my mind today and all those faces that I keep seeing in my memories. All the people I love, care for and miss. Please help those who have helped me, those who have shown me kindness, those strangers I remember from time to time, those strangers I have forgotten, those people that live in my good memories that make me believe in humanity again.

Please Allah, I know You know everything but I am forgetful. My heart reminds me sometimes of names and faces who have made me smile. I have long forgotten, but please let me remember them in my duas. Please accept my duas and protect those who have brought even the smallest happiness into my life. I have no means to help them as they have helped me, so please help them in their matters, as nothing is impossible for You.

@coffeewithajila

Dua:

No Muslim person says it, for any situation whatsoever, except that Allah Most High answers his call. *(Tirmidhi)*

La ilaha illa Anta, Subhanaka, inni kuntu mina z-zalimin.

There is no deity but You. Glory be to You! Verily, I have been among the wrongdoers.

Quran 21:87

Chapter Three

Emotional Intelligence

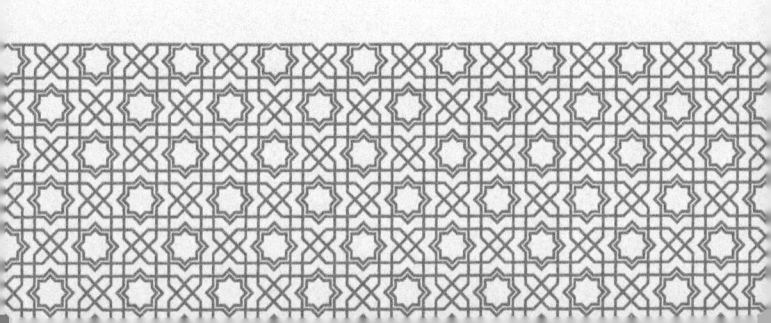

Al-Hakim is the Most Wise. He possess all the knowledge and, as al-Nabulsi states:

He does the proper thing in the proper way in the proper place and the proper time.

Whenever Allah decrees something in our lives, we must have certainty that it has been decreed with all His knowledge and His wisdom. So, whenever things do not go our way, or as we assumed they would, we need to put our trust in the One who truly knows what is best. How many of us can look back and see that a hardship, a closed door, or a painful memory, actually ended up providing some benefit in the long term? And even if we cannot see the wisdom now, our knowledge of this name should instill in us the conviction that there truly is wisdom and we will come to know it, whether in this life or the next.

Jinan Yousef (2023) p.208-209

Pure happiness is ultimately found in our contemplations of life.
To recognise that what we have is enough, there will never be another moment we feel that we have nothing.

mindofserenity

The word fitra comes from a root word meaning *"to split or bring forth"*. This implies that our work on this Earth is to split the shell of our ego and bring forth the divine seeds God has already planted in the garden of our spirits through the generosity of His love.

The firta is the innate disposition to believe in God, worship Him, and believe in His oneness.

Regardless of what our parents or any other person chooses to believe, the fitra or belief in God's oneness (tawhid) is part of the hardware of all human beings. While the software of our minds can be encoded in different ways based on life experience and environment, the hardware of the fitra cannot be changed.

A Helwa (2020) p.35

This being human is a guest house.
Every morning is a new arrival.
A joy, a depression, a meanness, some momentary
awareness comes as an unexpected visitor...
Welcome and entertain them all. Treat each guest
honorably.
The dark thought, the shame, the malice, meet them
at the door laughing and invite them in.
Be grateful for whoever comes, because each has been
sent as a guide from beyond.

Rumi.

Whoever curbs his anger while being able to act upon it, Allah will fill his heart with contentment.

Sahih al-Bukhari (6116)

A man once came to Mullah Nasruddin, and said, 'I am rich but depressed. I have taken all the money I own and have gone in search of happiness, but I have yet to find it.' As the man was staring toward the sky in reflection, the Mullah grabbed his bag of money out of his hands and ran away.

The man ran after the Mullah, screaming, "You thief! You thief!" The Mullah ran around a sharp corner and left the bag in the street, where the man would find it, and hid behind a pillar. When the man saw his bag on the ground his facial expression changed from despair to joy as he hugged his bag in pure bliss and happiness. After a few moments the Mullah came out of hiding and said, 'Sometimes you have to lose what you have and find it again for you to know the value of the blessing that you have always owned.'

Mullah Nasruddin.

"What is my purpose in life?" I asked the void.

"What if I told you that you fulfilled it when you took an extra hour to talk to that kid about his life?" Said the voice. "Or when you paid for that young couple in that restaurant? Or when you saved that dog in traffic? Or when you tied your father's shoes for him?

Your problem is that you equate purpose with goal based achievements. God or the universe or morality isn't interested in your achievements ... just your heart.

When you choose to act out of kindness, compassion, and love, you are already aligned with your true purpose. No need to look any further."

notetoselfphilosophy.com

The Prophet (pbuh) told us that 'the best of people are those that bring most benefit to the rest of mankind' and that 'if Allah wants good for a person then He uses him'

Jinan Yousuf (2023)

Picture your desires as vibrant butterflies. The more you try to grasp them tightly, the more they flutter away. But when you open your hands and let them rest, they may just choose to stay. Similarly, when you release the tight grip on your desires and surrender to Allah's will, you create space for the divine miracles to manifest into your life.

Zahra Pedersen (2023) p.74

If a man knows not his own soul, which is the nearest thing to him, what is the use of his claiming to know others?

It is as if a beggar who has not the wherewithal for a meal should claim to be able to feed a town.

Imam Al-Ghazali.

Show gentleness (rifq), for if gentleness is found in anything , it beautifies it and when it is taken out from anything it damages it.

Sunan Abi Dawud (4809)

Do not be envious
of some ones joy.

It might be their first time
to breathe out
after their lungs were drenched
in sorrow for too long

@ibtasempoetry

Hasan al-Basri was asked:

"Why do you appear unconcerned with what people say about you?"

He said, "When I was born I was born alone, when I shall die I will die alone, when I am placed in my grave I will be alone, and when I am taken to account before God I shall be alone. If I then enter the Fire it will be alone. And if I enter Paradise it will be alone. So what business do I have with people?"

Habib Ali Al-Jifri.

The most beloved people to Allah are those who are most beneficial to people. The most beloved deed to Allah is to make a Muslim happy, or remove one of his troubles, or forgive his debt, or feed his hunger.

That I walk with a brother regarding a need is more beloved to me than that I seclude myself in this mosque in Medina for a month.

Whoever swallows his anger, then Allah will conceal his faults. Whoever suppresses his rage, even though he could fulfil his anger if he wished, then Allah will secure his heart on the Day of Resurrection.

Whoever walks with his brother regarding a need until he secures it for him, then Allah Almighty will make his footing firm across the bridge on the day when the footings are shaken.

Al-Muʿjam al-Awsaṭ lil-Ṭabarānī (6026)

The Prophet (pbuh) taught us not to 'belittle any good deed, even meeting your brother with a cheerful face'

Sahih Muslim (2626)

An important part of our knowledge of God arises from the study and contemplation of our own bodies, which reveal to us the power, wisdom and love of the Creator.

His power, in that from a mere drop He has built up the wonderful frame of man; His wisdom is revealed in it's intricacies and the mutual adaptability of it's parts; and His love is shown by His not only supplying such organs as are absolutely necessary for existence, as the liver, the heart and the brain but those which are not absolutely necessary, as the hand, the foot, the tongue and the eye.

To these He has added as ornaments, the blackness of the hair, the redness of the lip and the curve of the eyebrow.

Imam Al-Ghazali.

Any one who will look into the matter will see that happiness is necessarily linked with the knowledge of God.

Each faculty of ours delights in that for which it was created.

Lust delights in accomplishing desire, anger in taking vengeance, the eye in seeing beautiful objects and the ear in hearing harmonious sounds.

The highest function of the soul of man is the perception of truth; in this accordingly it finds it's special delights.

Iman Al-Ghazali.

The finest souls are those who gulped pain
and avoided making others taste it.

Nizar Qabbani.

The 5 sensory pleasures of the world: drink, food, scent, cloth and sexuality. The highest drink is water, it's the least of things of the world, the highest food is the vomit of bees (honey), the highest cloth is the excrement of worms (silk), the highest smell is the mucous of a gazelle (musk) and the greatest pleasure in the world is the meeting of the two urinary tracts. That can't be real happiness

Al- Ghazali's (1963)

Dua:

Allah will grant whoever recites this seven times in the morning or evening whatever he desires from this world or the next.

Hasbiyallaahu laa 'ilaaha 'illaa Huwa 'alayhi tawakkaltu wa Huwa Rabbul-'Arshil-'Adheem.

Allah is sufficient for me. There is none worthy of worship but Him. I have placed my trust in Him, He is Lord of the Majestic Throne.

Ibn As-Sunni (no. 71)

Chapter Four

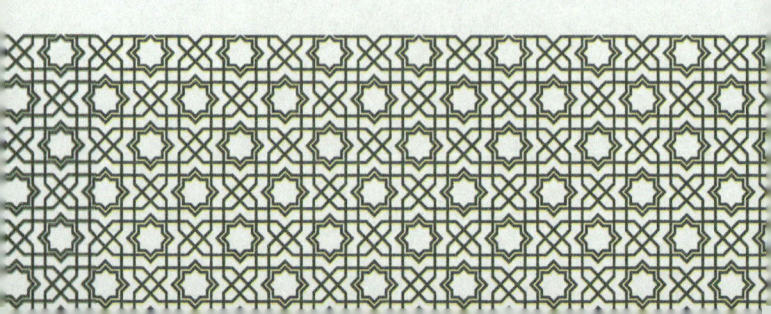

Staying Hopeful

God's Name Al-Jabbar indicates both majesty as well as beauty. The Arabic root of the word is *jim-ba-ra*, which gives rise to meanings such as to compel, to be strong, as well as to mend what is broken.

The Arabic word for a splint that is used to help a broken bone to heal is a *jibeera*, which is from the same root as *jabbar*. The splint compels the bone to heal in the right way and restore it to its whole, unbroken state.

Jinan Yousef (2023) p.119- 120.

May flowers grow in the saddest parts of you.

Zainab Aamir.

The God who made the stars, the seas, the mountains and its peaks, the universe and its galaxies felt this world would be incomplete without you and without me. Do you see how you are a puzzle piece in the whole - how without you here, there would be no hole? Your body is not just a clay tent that you live in, it's a piece of the universe you have been given. You are not a small star, you are a reflection of the entire cosmos. Can you hear the big bang in your heart? Eighty times a minute God knocks on the doors of your chest to remind you that He has never left, and that He is closer to you than the jugular vein in your neck (50:16). Every moment is divinely blessed, for this moment God is blowing the breath of life through eight billion different human chests. You are not just star dust and dirt, you are a reflection of God's beauty on Earth. You are not this mortal body that death will one day take. You are an everlasting spirit held in the mortal embrace of clay. You are not a human being meant to be spiritual, you are a spiritual being living this human being miracle.

Aru Barzak.

The Prophet (pbuh) tells us that, 'The one who (regularly) says seek forgiveness, God will relieve him of every burden, and make from every discomfort an outlet, and He will provide for him from (sources) he never could imagine'

Abu Dawud (1873)

In the intricate paths of life when difficulties and hardships confront a man, and the darkness of difficulty and suffering becomes long, it is patience only that acts like a light for a Muslim, that keeps him safe from wandering here and there and saves him from the muddy marsh of disappointment, desperation and frustration.

Iman Al-Ghazzali.

When you raise your hands to ask,
know that it is a sign that He wants to
give you.

When your eyes well up with regrets,
know that it is a sign that He wants to
forgive you.

He reached out to you before you
turned to Him.

themusingmuslim.

A young boy came across a butterfly cocoon and brought it into his house. He watched, over the course of hours, as the butterfly struggled to break free from its confinement. It managed to create a small hole in the cocoon, but its body was too large to emerge. It tired and became still.

Wanting to help the butterfly, the boy snipped a slit in the cocoon with a pair of scissors. But the butterfly was small, weak, and its wings crumpled. The boy expected the insect to take flight, but instead it could only drag its undeveloped body along the ground. It was incapable of flying.

The boy, in his eagerness to help the butterfly, stunted its development. What he did not know was that the butterfly needed to go through the process of struggling against the cocoon to gain strength and fill its wings with blood. It was the struggle that made it stronger.

Frank Dupree (2013)

While a man was walking on a road, he found a thorny branch in the road and he moved it aside. Allah appreciated his deed and forgave him.

Tirmidhi (1958)

Do not let your difficulties fill you with anxiety after all, it is only in the darkest nights that the stars shine more brilliantly.

Ali Ibn Abu Talib, unverified.

I know now that Allah was teaching me in those moments that it wasn't human beings that I needed.

Not a single soul knows what I know or feels exactly how I feel. He is the All-Knowing, so He knows better than anyone what my heart struggles with each day. He is the All-Seeing, so He sees what I hide away from the world. He is the All- Hearing, so He hears all my desperate pleas in the darkness of night.

From the little I know about Allah, I am satisfied. His promises are the absolute truth. If I do not leave Him, He is the only one who will never leave me.

What better friend or companion could I possibly have?

unknown.

Kintsugi is the remarkable Japanese art of repairing broken pottery:

Kin = Golden
Tsugi = Joinery

Kintsugi teaches that the broken pieces of an accidentally smashed pot should be carefully picked up, reassembled and glued together with lacquer inflected with the most expensive gold powder.

There should be no attempt to disguise the damage. The point is to render the fault lines beautiful and strong: the precious veins of gold emphasize that breaks have a philosophical merit all of their own.

In an age that prizes youth and perfection, Kintsugi retains a particular wisdom as applicable to our own lives as that as pots.

The care and love expended to shattered pieces should also encourage us to respect what is damaged and scared, vulnerable and imperfect, starting with ourselves and those around us.

School of Life.

When Allah tests you, it is never intended to destroy you. When He removes something in your possession, it is only in order to empty your hands for an even greater gift.

Ibn al-Qayyim

I do believe despair is a valid feeling, I do not believe, however, that it should define our lives. Some darkness is important for the light to be truly appreciated. In that sense, despair is a doorway, not a dead end. It creates in us an ache for hope. And it's that ache for hope that should define us.

"Do not grieve; indeed Allah is with us."

themusingmuslim

There is no Muslim who calls upon Allah, without sin or cutting family ties, but that Allah will give him one of three answers: He will quickly fulfil his supplication, He will store it for him in the Hereafter, or He will divert an evil from him similar to it." They said, "In that case we will ask for more." The Prophet said, "Allah has even more."

Musnad Aḥmad (11133)

Sorrow prepares you for joy. It violently sweeps everything out of your house, so that new joy can find space to enter. It shakes the yellow leaves from the bough of your heart, so that fresh, green leaves can grow in their place. It pulls up the rotten roots, so that new roots hidden beneath have room to grow. Whatever sorrow shakes from your heart, far better things will take their place.

Rumi.

The Messenger of Allah, peace and blessings be upon him, said,

"Verily, Allah Almighty loves to see the traces of blessings on his servant. He does not love one who wallows in misery and pessimism."

Al-Muʻjam al-Kabīr (5167)

All these people you are concerned about,
Did they create you?

Al- Ghazali.

Whoever wakes up safely in his home and is healthy in his body and has provisions for this day, would have acquired all the worldly possessions he is in need of.

Tirmidhi (2346)

Each moment contains a hundred messages from God.

To every cry of "Oh God."

He answers a hundred times "I am here."

"Do not loose heart or grieve" (3:139)

Because even in the depths of your darkest nights your Lord is with you always, saying,

"I am near" (2:186)

A.Helwa (2020) p.8

Dua:

Allahumma la sahla illa maa ja'altahu sahlan, wa Anta taj'alu l-hazna idha shi'ta sahla.

"O Allah! There is no ease except that which You make easy, and indeed You, when You want, make difficulties easy."

Sahih Ibn Hibban.

References by Chapter

chronologically listed.

Direct From the Golden Source:

1. *The Holy Qur'an*

Allah's Mercy:

1. Yousef, J. (2023) *Reflecting on the Names of Allah*, Al Burj Press.
2. Ibn Taymiyyah, T. *Majmoo' al-Fataawa* (Vol. 16)
3. Muslim, I. *Sahih Muslim* (Book 37, Hadith 6629).
4. *Sunan Abī Dāwūd* (5124)
5. *Sunan al-Tirmidhī* (3540)
6. *Al-Targhib* (Vol. 2, p. 227)
7. Maryam Amir, @themaryamamir.
8. Sulieman, O. (2020) *40 on Justice*, Kube Publishing Ltd.
9. Yousef, J. (2023) *Reflecting on the Names of Allah*, Al Burj Press.
10. Themusingmuslim, via Tumblr..
11. *Sunan al-Tirmidhī* (3556)
12. *Sahih Bukhairi* (Book 97, Hadith 126)
13. @blessedexpressions, via Instagram.
14. Suliman, O. (2024). Episode 3. In *Ramadan 2024 series*, Yaqeen institute.
15. Ibn Hajar al-Asqalani. *Fath al-Bari*.
16. *Sahih Muslim* (Book 50, Hadith 1)
17. *Sunan al-Tirmidhī* (3548)
18. Al-Munajjid, M. (2003) *Weakness of Iman*, Daar us-Sunnah Publisher.
19. @coffeewithajila, via Tumblr.
20. Quran 21:87

Emotional Intelligence:
1. *Yousef, J. (2023) Reflecting on the Names of Allah, Al Burj Press.*
2. *Mindofserenity, Via Instagram*
3. *Helwa, A .(2020) Secrets of Divine Love, Naulit Publishing House.*
4. *Chishty, S. (2022) Wisdom of Sufis: Quotes of Sufis to Attain Wisdom, Peace and Hope in Life, Pencil.*
5. *Sahih Bukhairi (Book 78, Hadith 143)*
6. *Shah, I., 2000. Tales of Mulla Nasrudin: For Children of All Ages. 18th ed. London: Octagon Press. (New World Literature Series).*
7. *notetoselfphilosophy.com (2020)*
8. *Yousef, J. (2023) Reflecting on the Names of Allah, Al Burj Press.*
9. *Z, Pedersen (2023) Manifesting Muslimah, KDP.*
10. *Al-Ghazali. (2016) The Alchemy of Happiness, Azafran Books.*
11. *Sunan Abī Dāwūd (Book 43, Hadith 37)*
12. *@ibtasempoetry, Via Instagram*
13. *@Quranandhadithh, via Twitter.*
14. *al-Ṭabarānī, A. al-Mu'jam al-Awsaṭ (no. 6026)*
15. *Sahih Muslim (Book 45, Hadith 187)*
16. *Al-Ghazali. (2016) The Alchemy of Happiness, Azafran Books.*
17. *Al-Ghazali. (2016) The Alchemy of Happiness, Azafran Books.*
18. *Qabbani, N. (1999) Arabian Love Poems: Full Arabic and English Texts, Lynee Rienner.*
19. *Al-Ghazali, A.H. (1963) Mīzān al-'Amal.*
20. *Ibn As-Sunni (no. 71)*

Staying Hopeful:
1. *Yousef, J. (2023) Reflecting on the Names of Allah, Al Burj Press.*
2. *Zaynab Aamir, Via Instagram – themotivationjournals*
3. *Helwa, A .(2020) Secrets of Divine Love, Naulit Publishing House.*
4. *Sunan Abī Dāwūd (Book 19, Hadith 5)*
5. *Al-Ghazali (2016) The Alchemy of Happiness, Azafran Books.*

6. Themusingmuslim, via Tumblr.
7. Dupree, F. (2013) Metamorphosis: The Transformation of a Soul, CreateSpace Independent Publishing Platform.
8. Sunan al-Tirmidhī (Book 27, Hadith 64)
9. Ali Ibn Abu Talib, unknown and unverified.
10. Unknown source, via Tumblr.
11. The School of Life (2016) Eastern Philosophy– Kintsugi via Youtube.
12. 11.Al-Qayyim (2017) The Sayings of Ibn Qayyim Al-Jawziyyah, Amazon Digital Services LLC - KDP Print US.
13. Themusingmuslim, via Tumblr.
14. Musnad Aḥmad, 11133.
15. Chishty, S. (2022) Wisdom of Sufis: Quotes of Sufis to Attain Wisdom, Peace and Hope in Life, Pencil.
16. Al-Mu'jam al-Kabīr, 5167
17. Al-Ghazali (2016) The Alchemy of Happiness, Azafran Books.
18. Sunan al-Tirmidhī (Book 36, Hadith 43)
19. Helwa, A .(2020) Secrets of Divine Love, Naulit Publishing House.
20. Sahih Ibn Hibban.

Printed in Great Britain
by Amazon